Leeds Castle

an illustrated guide

ANGELO HORNAK AND JONATHAN KEATES

Romantic, eventful and sensational, the story of Leeds Castle often resembles the story of England itself, and many of the makers of the nation's history figure in the annals of this unique place. The incomparable beauty of its site, on an island in a lake, amid a wooded, rolling landscape whose components have altered little during the centuries, never fails to charm and surprise the visitor, and it is precisely this strong natural allure that has allowed Leeds to survive and flourish in an age which has spelt destruction to many another English castle or country house.

There has been a wooden castle here since the ninth century and a stone one since 1130. Hamon de Crèvecoeur, a companion of William the Conqueror, had been granted the manor by the King, and his son, Robert, built a keep and a gatehouse. Of this the vaulted cellar under the main building survives, together with the lower masonry of the oldest tower of the castle, the Gloriette on its little island. In 1139, during the bitter struggle between King Stephen and his cousin the Empress Matilda, rivals for the throne, the King took Leeds from the Earl of Gloucester, Matilda's bastard brother, damaging the gatehouse in the process. The Crèvecoeurs continued work on the castle throughout their tenure, which lasted until

1268, when another Robert de Crèvecoeur, great-grandson of the original builder, was dispossessed of the manor for siding with Simon de Montfort in his rebellion against Henry III. It was during this period that the present enormous moat was formed from the marshes beside the river Len.

In exchange for the manor of Trottiscliffe, Robert had yielded Leeds to the King's friend Roger de Leyburn, whom Henry had made Sheriff of Kent and Cumberland, Warden of the Cinque Ports and Constable of Carlisle Castle.

His son William is portrayed for us, with epigrammatic brilliance, by an anonymous poet describing the siege of Caerlaverlock Castle in 1301, as 'a valiant man without a "but" or an "if" '. Such downrightness seems, alas, to have been unavailing against financial embarrassment, for in a document dated 1281 we read that he owed Agyn, a moneylender and arch-presbyter of the English Jews, the sum of 1,200 marks. It was surely Leeds' delightful setting, reminiscent of the moated castles of her homeland and its convenience as a lodging on royal routes from the south coast to London which prompted Eleanor of Castile, Edward I's queen, to purchase the castle, thus beginning a long association with English queens. The charter conveying the manor survives, dated 22nd June, 1278. Thus began 300 years of royal ownership of Leeds Castle and its links with the royal families of Europe. Edward's mother came from Provence and his Queen from Spain.

Edward and Eleanor immediately undertook extensive repairs, including building a series of bastions along the curtain walls, a bath under

The **wine cellar** under the kitchens is one of the surviving portions of the earlier Leeds Castle, built by Robert de Crèvecoeur during the early twelfth century.

In a room in the Gate Tower is a display of **antique dog collars** from various ages and countries, to fit the necks of every sort of animal from hound to lap dog. No museum in this country or elsewhere has a comparable collection.

the Maidens' Tower (a legacy, perhaps, of the sophisticated washing habits prevailing at the court of Eleanor's father, King Alfonso of Castile), a new Gate Tower and a chapel in the Gloriette. The chapel itself (reconsecrated as a Chapel Royal in our own day by the Archbishop of Canterbury, on 26th May, 1978) became a chantry in which, following Eleanor's death in 1290, prayers were ordered to be said for her soul, by a Letters Patent of the disconsolate King. Nine years later the castle was to figure once more as a royal residence, when Edward granted it to his second wife, Margaret of France, with whom he had spent his honeymoon here after their marriage at Canterbury.

A far more famous queen-consort, Isabella, the 'she-wolf' of France, wife of Edward II, tried to gain entrance to the castle in 1321 under the guise of seeking a night's lodging on a pilgrimage to Canterbury. Edward had recently granted Leeds to Sir Bartholomew de Badlesmere, whose castellan Thomas Colepeper (ancestor of later lords of the manor) sent the Queen packing. Despite coolness between King and consort, the insult was not to go unavenged. A tremendous force was summoned from Kent and the neighbouring counties and, led by the King in person, kept up the siege for

nearly a fortnight until the garrison surrendered. Lady Badlesmere and her children were sent to the Tower, Colepeper and his confederates, forfeiting their lands, were hanged from the Gate Tower, and Badlesmere himself, siding with rebellious barons in the north, was later captured and executed. Isabella appropriated the castle, which remained hers until her death in 1358.

Leeds was once again rebuilt, this time by William of Wykeham, Chancellor of England, founder of Winchester College and New College, Oxford, and one of the most forceful personalities of his age. During this period the manor, according to custom, was settled on Philippa, wife of Edward III, and it was in the eventful reign of her grandson Richard II that Leeds was visited by the great chronicler of European chivalry Jean Froissart, who arrived at the 'fair palace in the county of Kent' in July, 1395. A first edition of his chronicles with its record of his visit to Leeds is kept at the castle.

Shakespeare has perfectly crystallized Richard's disastrous reign and that of his cousin, the usurper Henry IV, who gained the throne at the cost of much personal happiness and security. He and his second wife Joan of Navarre sought refuge at Leeds from a summer plague epidemic in 1403, and Joan herself was to live at the castle in high style, as we find from details of her surviving household accounts. We note entries for cinnamon at 3s. 10d., ginger at 9s. 2d., black ribbon at 3s. 6d., 1,000 pins at 3d. a hundred, 3 dozen socks at 7d. a pair, the Queen's offerings in the chapel at 6s. 8d., and an average weekly expense of £13.

Joan was later accused of witchcraft for which she was sentenced to solitary confinement in Pevensey Castle, and to confiscation of her goods. The charges seem to have been trumped up by her confessor Randolph, at the instigation of her stepson Henry V, embarrassed for money and eager to provide for his new bride Katherine de Valois. Joan was released shortly before Henry's death in 1422.

Another suspected royal witch was actually tried in the chapel at Leeds on 21st October, 1441. She was Eleanor Cobham, wife of Humphrey, Duke of Gloucester. The Duke, founder of the university library at Oxford and a capable regent of England for the young Henry VI, was unpopular with the fretful, contentious nobles, many of whom were his relatives and thus bitterly jealous of his political power. The charges against Duchess Eleanor seem to have been partly true, though records of the trial do not survive.

Over succeeding decades Leeds was to have a more peaceful existence, in which its character as a palace rather than a castle grew more apparent. Henry VIII was quick to appreciate this, when in 1512 he appointed Sir Henry Guilford as constable. Guilford, a personal friend of the King's, who had been employed on diplomatic missions and campaigned with Henry in France, also found time to correspond with Erasmus and to have his portrait painted by Holbein. As constable he was empowered to supervise extensions and improvements to the castle, including the addition of an upper storey to the Gloriette, and the Maidens' Tower to house royal maids-of-honour, among whom, probably, was Anne Boleyn.

It was to another friend of Henry's, Sir Anthony St Leger, Lord Deputy of Ireland, that Leeds passed in 1552, since when it has never again belonged to the crown. St Leger's great-grandson, Sir Warham, ruined himself as a financial backer of Raleigh's fatal expedition to Guyana in search of the legendary El Dorado, and was forced to sell the estate to a kinsman, Sir Richard Smith, in exchange for his manor of Salmeston in the Isle of Thanet. In 1632, however, Smith's sisters sold Leeds to Sir Thomas Colepeper of Hollingbourne from whom it came to John, M.P. for Kent.

John Colepeper was an immensely astute politician, trusted by Charles I to give him accurate advice in his dealings with Parliament. A proud, ambitious man, who became Chancellor of the Exchequer and Master of the Rolls, he was created a baron in 1644, and eventually designated political adviser to the young Prince Charles. In 1660, the prince, as the restored King Charles II, returned Leeds to Colepeper and made him one of the proprietors of an enormous grant of land in the American colony of Virgina. The area comprised a stretch of territory as big as all the Home Counties put together (some five million acres) between the Potomac and Rappahannock rivers, part of which is now covered by the southern sector of Washington D.C.

Colepeper, or Culpeper as it was later spelt, died soon after the grant was made, and his son Thomas inherited his baronial title, his estates and much of his skill in manoeuvring others. During his absence from Leeds as Governor of the Isle of Wight, the castle was used as a prison for captured French and Dutch sailors. In charge of these was the Kentish diarist John Evelyn, who seems to have found the 'famous hold' in need of repair and proper drains. Culpeper, however, returned to Leeds in 1667 and eight years afterwards was appointed Governor of Virginia, where his behaviour in bending the laws to his own convenience was as high-handed as it had apparently been on the Isle of Wight. The Fairfax Hall, an old tithe barn, dates from the period of his arrival in Virginia.

While in Virginia he had contrived to buy out his co-owners of the proprietary grant, leaving most of his estates at his death in 1688 to his daughter Katherine, wife of the impecunious Thomas, Lord Fairfax. To their son the Proprietary proved an even greater financial incentive. Having tried and failed at his father's remedy of marrying an heiress, he set off in 1735 for Virginia to establish his claims against the colonial government to sole authority on his American lands. When this was confirmed in 1745, he settled at Belvoir, on the banks of the Potomac, as the doyen of the planter aristocracy and a model landowner. Later, in moving closer to the colony's frontier, he called his new property 'the Manor of Leeds' to remind him of the Kentish estate he had given to his brother Robert.

As surveyor of the Proprietary's western fringes, Fairfax had employed the young George Washington, whose brother Lawrence had married

Fairfax's cousin Anne and had come to live at Mount Vernon, granted to his family by Thomas Colepeper in the previous century. George Washington, the love of whose life was Sally Fairfax, wrote of Belvoir that 'the happiest moments of my life were spent there' and sincerely regretted Lord Fairfax's death in 1782, calling him 'the good old Lord'.

Leeds itself, meanwhile, had been 'improved' in the eighteenth-century manner, with what Horace Walpole styled 'a gleam of Gothic', by Robert Fairfax, who welcomed George III and Queen Charlotte here in 1778, while they were reviewing troops encamped near Maidstone. At Fairfax's death the property passed to his nephew, Denny Martin, and thence to the Wykeham-Martin family, who did so much to restore the castle's essentially mediaeval character.

Today Leeds Castle is the centre for a charitable foundation devoted to encouraging medical research throughout the world. Its existence as such is owing to its last private owner, Olive, Lady Baillie, who bought the castle in 1926. Captivated, as women of earlier centuries had been, by the beauties of Leeds, she undertook a painstaking restoration of the fabric, both within and without, thus making it an ideal setting in which she could welcome members of the royal family, politicians and diplomats. Visitors to Leeds will notice the prevailing theme, in the decoration, of exotic birds, reflecting an interest of Lady Baillie's matched in the splendid aviaries still maintained today. Hers too was the creation, from a swampy morass, of the enchanting Wood Garden. At her death in 1974, it could well be said that her affectionate guardianship of the castle, its moat and parkland, had been more effective than any other in preserving for us the singular charm of what has been called 'the loveliest castle in the world'.

Portrait of Lady Baillie and her two daughters

The machicolated **Gate Tower** of Leeds Castle bore the brunt of both the attack by King Stephen in 1139, and the siege by King Edward II almost two centuries later, after which the rebellious castellan Thomas Colepeper was hanged here. Most of the masonry dates from the end of the fourteenth century, perhaps the finest period of English castle building.

A fourteenth-century iron key recovered from the mud near the Gate Tower when the moat was cleaned in 1823.

The oldest part of the castle is the Gloriette. On the walls of the **Chambre de Madame la Reine** hang Brussels tapestries, two of them illustrating the story of King Hezekiah from the Second Book of Kings, and a third showing the story of Hercules and the Cretan bull. This seventh of his ten labours involved the hero's capture of a bull driven mad by the god Poseidon as a revenge on King Minos of Crete, who had refused to sacrifice the bull. Bearing it home to Greece in triumph, Hercules then turned it loose to run wild through the countryside.

Lucas Cranach: *Adam and Eve*

Dominated by its heavy conical chimneypiece, the
Chambre de Retrait is enlivened by a Flemish
tapestry.

The **Fountain Court** inside the Gloriette has been
supplied by water from a spring since the time of
Edward III.

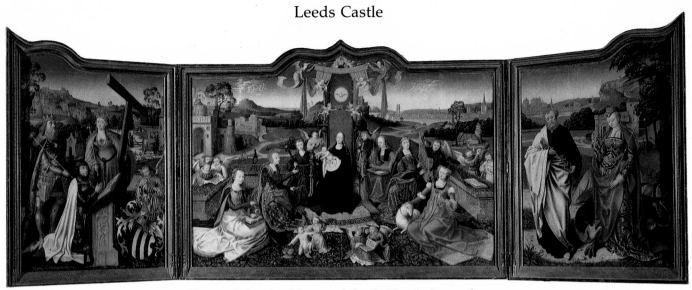

Tryptych by the Master of the S. Ursula Legend

The **Great Chamber** leading into the fountain court has several examples of oak furniture from different periods. A long seventeenth-century table supports the brilliantly detailed **triptych** by the Master of the S. Ursula Legend, who flourished in Bruges during the late fifteenth and early sixteenth centuries. The Virgin, enthroned amid a retinue of saints and angels, sits in a typical *hortus conclusus* of the late Middle Ages, with SS. Margaret and Peter in the right hand panel, and the knightly donor on the left, attended by S. Helena with the True Cross, and by one of the Holy Roman Emperors. The painting is said to have been presented to a church in Cologne in 1515.

Van Dyck: *Princess Elizabeth and Princess Anne,* the two youngest children of Charles I

The Henry VIII **banqueting hall** runs a length of 75 feet between the chapel and the gallery along the western side of the castle. The bow window is one of several features dating from Sir Henry Guilford's supervision of rebuilding for Henry VIII in 1512. Other noteworthy aspects include the Renaissance chimneypiece adorned with medallion busts in relief, and the refectory table from a monastery near Chartres dating from the early seventeenth century. Above it hangs a magnificent carpet made to Persian designs in the Mughal India of about the year 1600. In one of the windows stands the **figure of S. Barbara**, a French mediaeval stone carving. The patron saint of gunners, sappers and bombardiers, she is shown holding the tower in which she was imprisoned by her father before her martyrdom.

The **chapel**, recently reconsecrated for worship, contains a series of carved wooden panels, dating from the early sixteenth century and probably executed at Ulm. The lively details in the **Annunciation scene** recall similar treatments by painters of the same period: the Angel's upraised hand, the Virgin's gesture of self-effacing modesty, and her studious posture before a prie-dieu containing devotional works and a flagon, are all features typical of a northern European handling of this favourite theme from the Gospels. The silver cross on the altar was donated by the Royal College of Nursing.

Early sixteenth-century wooden panel of the Annunciation

The chapel **organ** is thought to have been built by Robert and William Gray in 1796 for Spencer Percival, the Prime Minister assassinated in 1812.

A wall of the **Fountain Court** with timber-framed walls.

The **gothic oak staircase**, with its fluted newel post, comes from France. On the landing at its head hangs a group of drawings by Constantin Guys. 'His business', says Baudelaire of Guys, 'is to separate from modern fashion whatever there may be in it of history; to extract the eternal from the ephemeral'. Born in 1802, Guys was a French army officer, whose talent for immediate graphic impressions of everyday scenes found an outlet in a series of pictures of the Crimean War drawn for the *Illustrated London News*. Later, in Paris, he turned to drawing and pen-and-wash sketches which brilliantly evoke the flamboyant, overdressed extravagance as well as the disreputable aspects of life during the Second Empire. As Baudelaire noted, Guys loved to portray his figures riding in their smart carriages, and by a grim paradox it was one of these which effectively put an end to his career when in 1855 he was knocked down and injured by a passing equipage.

Lithe and enigmatic in the best of feline traditions, this **bronze cat**, 2,500 years old, was designed as a mummy case in ancient Egypt of the Saite period (*c.* 600 BC). This was an age of prosperity for Egypt, ruled by the princes of Saïs in the Nile delta and warring successfully against neighbouring peoples, including the Israelites of the days of the Kings. Egyptian art of the period reflected a conscious nostalgia for the styles of earlier dynasties, so much so that it is often considered as a kind of 'Egyptian Renaissance'. The cat was sacred to Bast, goddess of joy, whose annual festival at Bubastis provided an excuse for drunken revels.

Leeds has two notable canvases by **Camille Pissarro (1831–1903)**. A visit to Rouen in 1896 produced a remarkable series of works, and two years later, though plagued by weakening eyesight, the painter returned to the city to complete three studies of the old Rue de l'Épicerie, prior to its demolition. One of these is at Leeds and is illustrated here. The other Pissarro at the castle, a snow scene, is one of several painted at Pontoise and Louveciennes near Paris in the early 1870s at the time of the invention of the Impressionist style. This was the period when Pissarro's canvasses acted as a powerful influence on the young Cézanne. Of his painting he once said 'I see only spots of colour. What I try first of all to capture is the essential relationship'.

Camille Pissarro: *View of Rouen*

Eugène Boudin: *Beach scene*

Henri de Toulouse-Lautrec: *Sketch of Gabrielle*

Henri Fantin-Latour: *Still life*

Eugène Boudin (1824–98) was an important precursor of
Impressionism and a friend of both Corot and Monet.
Born at Honfleur, the son of a pilot, he was chiefly
inspired by the changing seas and skies of his native
Normandy coast, and especially loved to paint scenes like
this one, on the beaches of such fashionable resorts as
Trouville.

An arresting presence among the conference room
Impressionists is that of **Toulouse-Lautrec**, represented
here in his sketch of Gabrielle, a lady of the Moulin Rouge,
a fascinating contrast, in its verve and energy, with the
reflective gentle canvases of his contemporaries Pisarro
and Vuillard.

Fantin-Latour is unique among French painters of the
nineteenth century for his love of flower subjects. In an
Impressionist idiom he managed superbly to renew the
tradition of the seventeenth-century Dutch masters, and
this still life composition of Aimée Vibert roses is a well
loved picture at Leeds. This rose is grown in the Culpeper
Garden.

Leeds Castle

A view along the corridor which links the
Gloriette to the later part of the castle.

The **staircase hall**, with its Romanesque Italian lion, Gothic arches and display of **hunting tapestries**, makes one of the most immediately striking ensembles at Leeds Castle.

The **floral still life** by J. B. Monnoyer offers an intriguing contrast with the Fantin-Latour in the conference room. Monnoyer (1636–1699) trained in Antwerp before entering the service of Louis XIV, for whom he worked at Versailles, Saint Cloud and Marly. In 1685 he came to England, at the invitation of the Duke of Montague, and was later employed by William III and Queen Mary at Kensington Palace.

Bowl, jug and dish from the mother-of-pearl collection formed by Lady Baillie

The **yellow drawing room** brings together a carpet said to have
been made by the monks at a St. Petersburg monastery for the
wedding of Catherine the Great to Tsar Peter of Russia, a mother-
of-pearl collection belonging to Lady Baillie and a pair of
eighteenth-century Japanese porcelain hawks. Over the fireplace
hangs Tiepolo's *Pulchinelli enjoying an alfresco meal* (see next page).
G. B. Tiepolo (1696–1770) was a prolific painter who worked in
Würzburg and Madrid and well as in his native Italy, and was
particularly well known for his frescoes employing an airy,
brilliant style. His paintings display the same characteristics,
including those featuring the Commedia del'Arte figure of
Pulchinella placed amid sharply observed scenes from
contemporary life. The backgrounds to these pictures are often
(as here) sinister and threatening skies, and the grotesque masks
and costumes of the clowns add an extra dimension of eeriness
which anticipates works by Goya.

G.B. Tiepolo: *Pulchinelli enjoying an alfresco meal*

J. F. Millet: *Shepherdess*

The **Thorpe Hall room** is an outstanding example of English mid-seventeenth-century decorative art. It was taken from a house near Peterborough, designed in 1653 by Peter Mills for Chief Justice St. John. Mills, commissioned with Wren, Pratt and May to supervise the rebuilding of London after the Fire of 1666, also designed this rich panelling, with its garlanded pilasters and frames supported on volutes.

Millet's painting of a little shepherdess among her flock hangs in the room. It belongs to the period during the mid-nineteenth century in which he concentrated on paintings of peasant subjects, and makes an interesting comparison with his more famous, if more sombre, shepherdess picture known as *La Grand Bergère*, whose exhibition in 1864 clinched his popularity with a French public which at first thought him too 'socialist' in his outlook on country life.

The **doorway** of the Thorpe Hall room, with its composition of volutes, pilasters, garlands and panels, typifies seventeenth-century English woodcarving at its best.

Doorway of the Thorpe Hall room

Italian stone lion

Detail from a Flemish hunting tapestry

The austere beauty of the stone-flagged **hall** is
dominated by **Flemish hunting tapestries**, in
which hounds and beasts of the chase crouch amid
woodland thickets, and by the pink **stone lion**
holding a ram in its paws. A familiar feature of the
Romanesque churches of northern Italy
(outstanding examples are at Parma Cathedral and
San Zeno in Verona), it originally formed the base
to one of the columns of a portico.

Details of the exterior of the castle

View from the roof of the castle with the flag bearing the arms of Lady Baillie

Leeds Castle